S0-ARE-548

because
two are
better
than one

for you, Grandma

---

with love,

---

date

Our purpose at Howard Publishing is to:

- *Increase faith* in the hearts of growing Christians
- *Inspire holiness* in the lives of believers
- *Instill hope* in the hearts of struggling people everywhere

Because He's coming again!

You and Me, Grandma © 2004 by Howard Publishing Co., Inc.
All rights reserved. Printed in Mexico
Published by Howard Publishing Co., Inc.
3117 North 7th Street, West Monroe, LA 71291-2227

04 05 06 07 08 09 10 11 12 13   10 9 8 7 6 5 4 3 2

Written by Judy Gordon
Edited by Between the Lines
Interior design by LinDee Loveland and Stephanie D. Walker
Photography by LinDee Loveland

ISBN: 1-58229-370-8

No part of this publication may be reproduced in any form without the prior written permission of the publisher except in the case of brief quotations within critical articles and reviews.

Scripture taken from the HOLY BIBLE, NEW INTERNATIONAL VERSION ®. Copyright © 1973, 1978, 1984 by International Bible Society. Used by permission of Zondervan. All rights reserved. The Lord's Prayer was taken from The Holy Bible, 21st Century King James Version ®. Copyright 1994 by Deuel Enterprises, Inc., Gary, SD 57237. All rights reserved.

because two are better than one

you
and
me

Grandma

HOWARD
PUBLISHING CO.
Printed in Mexico

Judy Gordon

You are to me a treasure whose
worth is beyond measure.

Grandma

The very fact that you don't look
or act or feel like the grandparents of
even a generation ago does not mean
that you are less, but that you are
more—in effect, an evolved form of
grandparents, primed to do a bigger
and more challenging job
than any group before you.

Arthur Kornhaber

Lavender Means Love

Megan caught a small whiff of something familiar as she walked through the cosmetics department in Macy's. It took her only a moment to identify the memory-laden scent. *Of course*, she thought. *Lavender*.

A store mirror beamed back the girlish smile that had spread across Megan's face, and she chuckled as she thought of her grandmother. From the quizzical look a clerk gave her, she could tell that her amusement didn't quite fit with her sleek navy business suit. But how could she not smile when she thought of Lucy Lavender?

Megan had grown up living next-door to her grandmother, Lucy. It hadn't always been easy being the granddaughter of a woman who was so in love with lavender that she wore it from her suede shoes to her hats with pale purple plumage. Add her rich red hair in contrast, and Megan's grandma was easy to spot in a crowd.

But that wasn't the worst part—she even drove a lavender car! Megan hadn't minded riding with Grandma Lucy in her grade-school days, but once she entered junior high, she often wriggled out of invitations to ride in the "lavender limo." That's what a classmate called it one day, and Megan couldn't rid her mind of the term or the mocking laughter that went with it.

At least her parents had been able to convince her grandmother not to paint her house lavender. She settled instead for lavender shutters and window boxes on her white house and lined the white picket fence with every variety of lavender flower or plant she could get her hands on.

It was learning about the plant itself that had sparked Lucy's love of lavender. No. That wasn't exactly true. It had begun with a special teacher.

Grandma Lucy told Megan the story one afternoon over a cup of lavender mint tea. "My first memories of my parents were of hardworking people who thought of life in terms of survival more than anything else. They dressed us four kids in mostly dark clothing that wouldn't show the dirt as much, because cleanliness wasn't a high priority.

"I thought all of that was normal until we moved to town, where I attended a new school. The kids made fun of me—telling me I was dirty and that I smelled bad." Her grandmother shook her head at the painful memory. "Thankfully, I had a caring teacher. Her name was Mrs. Sweet—yes, that really was her name—and not only was she a sweet lady, but she always smelled sweet too.

"She took me aside after school one day and gave me a little brown bag filled with all things lavender. I don't recall all the items now, but I know it had a bar of lavender soap and a plastic lavender comb. She told me that the dry leafy things inside a lace heart were from the lavender flower and that it was a sachet ladies put in dresser drawers to make their clothes smell good."

Megan's grandmother went on to tell her how she had gone to the school library and looked up everything she could find about the lavender plant. "Did you know, Megan, that it was originally called spikenard because of its long, pointed stems? In fact, it was the oil of lavender that Mary used on Jesus' feet. The name was changed when the Romans started using it in their baths. Their word for washing was *lavare*, and the plant became known as lavender."

Her grandmother paused. "I don't want to bore you with all of this, but once I started learning about the lavender plant, I couldn't stop. Did you know that it takes eighty pounds of lavender to make one ounce of oil? For centuries it has been used to treat all kinds of ailments—everything from curing headaches to calming nerves. Some people swear it keeps moths away from woolen clothing.

"Anyway, I washed every day with the lavender soap, and the kids stopped making fun of me. Mrs. Sweet continued to slip me little lavender things now and then, especially the soap, and I've never forgotten her for it. I always vowed that I would try to be like her—both

13

sweet smelling and sweet toward others."

Her grandmother laughed. "I never expected to get so carried away with the color though. I think it must have been because of Donnie Jones, a boy in high school I had a big crush on. He told me once how good the lavender sweater I was wearing looked with my red hair, and after that it seemed everything I bought was lavender. I never dreamed it would become my trademark!"

Megan grinned at her grandma. "Well, I may have your red hair, Grandma, but I know I'll never wear lavender like you do!"

Her grandmother returned the smile. "It doesn't matter if you wear the color, my dear girl. But I do hope you'll always be a sweet fragrance wherever you go, just like the light, refreshing scent of lavender."

But when Megan became a teenager, she didn't want anything to do with lavender—the scent or the color—and as much as she hated to admit it, sometimes even her grandmother. Megan loved Grandma Lucy, but why couldn't she just be normal like her friends' grandmas?

Then came the invitation in the mail addressed to her mom and Miss Megan Jackson. Her mom handed her the ecru envelope with a scalloped flap and lavender lining, and a faint fragrance escaped when Megan withdrew the printed card.

You are cordially invited to a
Lace and Lavender Tea
in honor of Lucy Lavender
on the occasion of her birthday.

Good grief, Megan thought. *They didn't even use her real last name!* The invitation went on to give the details of the surprise event hosted by one of her grandma's closest friends, Betty. It ended with "Please come dressed in lavender."

Megan groaned. "Mom, I don't have to wear lavender, do I? I don't even own anything that color!"

Her mother smiled as she opened her closet. "Oh, yes, you do!" Her triumphant grin and the shiny shopping bag in her hand told Megan what was coming next. "I just found the perfect thing for you when I was downtown a while ago." She pulled out an outfit from the bag and held it up, and Megan did have to admit it was pretty cool, in spite of the fact that it was lavender. She sighed. Well, at least none of her friends would be there to laugh at her.

On the Saturday of the tea, Betty gushed as she led Megan and her mother to the garden and patio area. "Megan, how lovely you look! I don't think I've ever seen you wear lavender. It complements your gorgeous hair and fair complexion just like it does your grandma's." Megan grimaced. As much as she wanted to help her grandma celebrate her birthday, she wanted even more to get out of lavender and back into her jeans. Then she could feel like herself again.

Several tables were donned with lace tablecloths, and lavender was everywhere—the dishes, the centerpieces of dried lavender bouquets and candles, and ecru place cards inscribed with lavender ink. The buffet table was laden with lavender offerings as well: lavender and orange salad, lavender biscuits, and pink lavender lemonade, to name a few.

Grandma Lucy's face lit up with surprise and delight as she greeted her guests and joined in the laughter and lively conversation.

Before serving the birthday cake iced with delicate lavender flowers, Betty announced a gift giving of a different kind—words of affirmation to celebrate Lucy Lavender. One by one, several women stood up and addressed Megan's grandma and shared what she meant to them.

"I remember when I was laid off from my job, you brought over a delicious meat loaf meal, topped off with chocolate cake. But most of all, your caring presence gave me comfort and courage."

"Thank you for the time you sewed Easter dresses for my two daughters when we were short on money. They still talk about their lavender dresses from the lavender lady."

"I will never forget how you drove me to the hospital when I went into early labor with my first child. I was so scared, and you knew exactly how to calm me."

Grandma Lucy's eyes glistened, and her face glowed. As Megan watched and listened, she began to see her grandma as someone besides the lady who was crazy about lavender. She saw a beautiful, caring person who had left a lingering fragrance of love in every life she touched.

The insights and memories Megan gathered that day at the Lace and Lavender Tea never left her. They're what made her turn around in Macy's and head back to the cosmetics counter to find the source of that lavender scent. She'd mail it to her grandma with a note on a lavender card: *Whenever I smell lavender, I think of sweet and special you. To me, lavender will always mean love.*

Ten Names for Grandma . . . for Love

1 *Nana*

2 *Grammy*

3 *Grams*

4 *Mama Grand*

5 *Gigi (as in GG for Great-Grandma)*

6 *Nonny*

7 *GSP (Grandma Sugar Plum)*

8 *Mamaw*

9 *Mema*

10 *Mugga (which made her mother Big Mugga)*

IN THE COOKIES OF LIFE GRANDMOTHERS ARE THE CHOCOLATE CHIPS

thank

you...

for your example of
resiliency and courage.

A Legacy of Laughter

If my grandma knew how to do anything, she knew how to laugh. She'd laugh at *I Love Lucy* reruns, no matter how many times she saw Lucy and Ethel stuffing their mouths with chocolates. She'd laugh at her cat when he'd go slip-sliding over her newly waxed floor. She even laughed at the corny elephant jokes I told her. (The only one she could ever remember was why elephants wear red toenail polish—so they can hide in a cherry tree!)

The thing I loved most about Grandma's laughter was her unabashed enthusiasm. She wasn't one to cover her mouth to suppress the giggles spilling out of her. Oh, no. She'd throw back her silver-crowned head to howl and then lift her wire-rimmed glasses to wipe away the laughter-induced tears. She simply couldn't contain her mirth.

I always think of Grandma when something tickles me so much that tears roll down my cheeks. Or when my face and sides ache from laughing so hard, I'm gasping for breath.

My kids have inherited this inability to contain laughter—especially when something funny happens in church. One will just be getting it under control when the other sputters a laugh out of the corner of his mouth, starting the convulsive waves all over again. What can I say? It's all Grandma's fault!

Thank you, dear Grandma, for the gift of your infectious laughter that continues to fill each generation with irrepressible joy.

Perfume and incense bring joy to

the heart, and the pleasantness of

one's friend springs from his

earnest counsel.

—Proverbs 27:9

My dear and wise grandma,

Do you know that you are more than a grandmother to me? You're also one of my dearest friends. It is to you I come for the best of everything: the best ideas, the best recipes, the best advice. And you always offer these things in the best of ways—with gentleness and kindness. No wonder I love you so much!

Your grateful (and getting wiser) grandchild

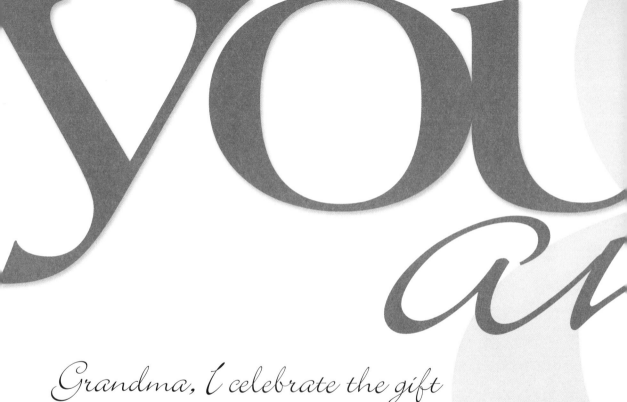

Grandma, I celebrate the gift of you—my confidante, my hope-giver, my dearest friend.

Grandma

Grandmothers are to life what the Ph.D. is to education. There is nothing you can feel, taste, expect, predict, or want that the grandmothers in your family do not know about in detail.

Lois Wyse

Grammy's Gift

Tricia stared at the stack of white envelopes toppling every which way onto the scarred oak kitchen table and sighed. Utility bills, medical bills, car insurance—and those made up only a portion of the pile. The extra medical and insurance bills couldn't have come at a worse time. She had so hoped to be able to surprise her husband, David, with something special for his birthday next week.

She sighed again and lifted her eyes to the room around her. Usually the splashy colors of her sunny kitchen with its pansy wallpaper would buoy her spirits. But not today. Her gaze fell on the wall hanging her grandmother had embroidered years ago for their wedding gift. In neat, even letters, Grammy had stitched the Bible verse "And now abides faith, hope and love, but the greatest of these is love."

Tricia smiled, remembering with fondness how much her grandmother had loved. Grammy had died five years ago, yet hardly a day passed that Tricia wasn't reminded of her and her loving ways. When Tricia made Grammy's apple-cinnamon muffins, she recalled all the times she saw those muffins carried to a neighbor who was ill or to a friend who just needed cheering up. The muffins would most likely be wrapped in a red cloth napkin or bandana, and often they were accompanied by a hearty pot of homemade soup. Grammy always said, "What warms the body warms the soul."

And what Grammy gave to others, Tricia knew, always warmed the soul: rainbow scarves knitted out of leftover lengths of yarn, raisin puff cookies still warm from the oven, or a book with her familiar, flowing handwriting on the front flyleaf: "This just made me think of you. Enjoy!" The book may have been bought at a yard sale, but it would be the perfect choice for its recipient. That was Grammy—always paying attention to people's needs and likes and always giving out of what little she had.

The final words on the wall hanging echoed in Tricia's heart and mind. "But the greatest of these is love." She could still hear Grammy's lilting voice after Tricia had hugged her and thanked her for the lovely present. "I hope you'll always remember, Tricia, the truth of those words. Love *is* the greatest of all. Love always makes a way."

Tricia shook her head, and yet another sigh escaped. She longed to believe her grandmother, but she didn't know how love was going to make a way this time. There was simply more month than money, and she'd be fortunate to even have money for the ingredients of David's favorite cake, German chocolate. Yet she yearned to do more than bake a cake—she wanted to give him at least one special gift.

The longing she had seen in David's deep blue eyes recently, as he examined a leather-bound classic at the local antique bookstore, was still etched in Tricia's mind. He hadn't said a word, but she knew it would be the perfect addition to the few but cherished volumes in his personal library. How she would love to see that expression of wistfulness turn to one of surprise and joy.

Get real, girl. You don't have two nickels to rub together right now, as Grammy would say. There's no way you can afford to buy anything extra. At times like these, Tricia wished she and David hadn't decided to get rid of all their credit cards. But they had learned the hard way about living on credit, and she knew she didn't want to go back to the lifestyle of buy now, pay later. This was hard, but that had been worse.

She pulled herself up in her chair and squared her shoulders for the task before her. Was it just her imagination or had the pile of bills grown larger? The bright white envelopes stood in stark contrast to the grayness of her spirits. *Oh, dear Grammy, how I wish you were here now. I could use a generous dose of your love and optimism.*

Her grandmother's words repeated themselves in Tricia's mind yet again: *"Love always makes a way." But how, Grammy, how?* She wished her grandmother could answer her plaintive question. More than anything, she wished Grammy were still alive. She'd give anything to see her smile and sparkling eyes light up a room again. Tricia also wished her children could have really known her; Justin was a toddler and Allison only an infant when Grammy died. Her grandmother had delighted in both babies and lavished on them her one-of-a-kind love. They still had the cuddly blankets she had knitted, one blue and one pink.

Sounds of excitement erupted from Allison's bedroom and interrupted Tricia's musings. Earlier the kids had asked for the dress-up suitcase, which Tricia kept filled with an assortment of fun attire she had picked up for next to nothing at garage sales. She stored it on a closet shelf to be pulled down for rainy days like today.

Curiosity drew her down the hall to see what was causing such a commotion when the kids spilled out of the bedroom.

"What's going on, you two?"

Allison's sky blue eyes danced, and her normally rosy cheeks were flushed even more than usual. Hands behind her back, she was bouncing like a little pogo stick, and her words burst out like explosions of popcorn. "Mommy, Mommy, do you remember that old brown wallet that's been in the dress-up suitcase forever?"

"What? What wallet?"

With Justin beaming beside her, Allison pulled her hands out from behind the fluffy pink dress she was wearing over her jeans and T-shirt and waved the small wallet in front of her mom.

Oh, yes. Now Tricia did remember. And she was amazed at the timing of the memory, since it involved her grandmother.

Seeing the wallet took her back to when she and David were first married. They had returned to their hometown in the Sierra Nevada for a family Labor Day picnic, but they were most excited about the backpacking trip they had planned for the week following the holiday. All the gear they had borrowed and bought, along with freeze-dried food and other provisions, were stowed in the back of their old Volkswagen van dubbed The Green Machine.

The morning of their departure dawned as clear as nearby Sabrina Lake, and amid a flurry of hugs from family members, they said their good-byes. After a quick stop at the gas station, they were on their way, and with each mile their anticipation rose to match the towering mountains in the distance. A couple of hours down the road, they decided to stop for a snack. Tricia dug around inside her purse for her wallet, but her hand couldn't find the familiar, solid lump.

She jumped out of the van and checked the floor and under the seat. "David, have you seen my wallet?" They had searched in every crevice of the vehicle when the scene at the gas station suddenly replayed in Tricia's mind. After she had given David the money for gas, she had leaned over to pull up the socks in her hiking boots. Then she had hopped back inside . . . and, she realized, left her wallet on the roof of the van.

"Oh, no!" she wailed, tears forming. "All of our money and credit cards are in my wallet." They had planned to buy their final food supplies at the last town before heading into the mountains. After discussing their options, she and David knew they really had only one. They turned around and drove back to her grandmother's house.

Grammy clucked her tongue in sympathy when she heard their tale of woe. She gave them both a hug, sat them down with some cookies and lemonade, and then disappeared into her bedroom. A few minutes later she returned with a small, brown wallet. "Here, Tricia, why don't you use this until you can get a new one?"

How just like Grammy. Tricia thanked her and tucked the wallet into her purse as she and David continued to list the credit card companies they needed to notify.

They returned home, but Tricia never needed to use the wallet her grammy had given her. Within days, a package had arrived in the mail—sent by the honest woman who had found the lost wallet. Tricia's grandmother rejoiced with them over the phone and said, "Well, I hope you got good use out of the wallet I gave you."

And now here was Tricia's daughter waving that long-forgotten wallet in front of her. *But why all the excitement?* Allison stopped jumping and plopped down on the carpet. With a dramatic flair, she opened the wallet and tugged at something in one of the little pockets. She grinned as she threw up a green bill and then another and another. Tricia stood in stunned silence as fifty dollars fell at her feet—enough to buy the book for David and some to spare. Her grandmother's words rang in her ears: *"Well, I hope you got good use out of the wallet I gave you."*

Tears clouded Tricia's eyes as she looked heavenward. *Oh, dear Grammy, thank you so much. Once again you've given the perfect gift. You were right—love always does make a way.*

Ten Things Grandma Always Said

1 *Pray about everything— even what to fix for dinner!*

2 *A clean conscience makes a soft pillow.*

3 *The Lord may not come when you want Him to, but He'll always be on time.*

4 *Eat your bread crusts so you'll be able to fight the bears.*

5 *Carrots are good for your eyes.*

6 *I love you more than pumpkin pie!*

7 *You can't have the cherries without the pits.*

8 *You do not hate anyone. You may dislike some people, but you do not hate them.*

9 *Yes, you can have it.*

10 *A good name is a second inheritance.*

thank

you...

for seeing not only what is
but also what can be.

Nobody Hurt

Grandma liked to quote several favorite sayings, but one has always stayed with me: "Nobody hurt." Only two little words, but I learned that those two words could change the color of a day from gloomy gray to sunny yellow. Grandma knew and practiced the truth behind the words *nobody hurt*; it was obvious she valued people more than things.

When my sister and I left our crayons in Grandma's car, and the summer sun melted them into the fabric of the backseat, Grandma shrugged and said, "Nobody hurt." When I spilled red punch on her new white tablecloth, she just scooped it up and said, "Nobody hurt." When my backward somersault cracked her crystal vase, my dear grandma only said, "Nobody hurt."

The gift of my grandmother's wise expression inspired me to have the same attitude with my sons. The task can be challenging, especially on days already filled with annoyances like spilled milk and muddy tracks. After all, the impromptu and enthusiastic wrestling match in our living room that tipped over and broke one of my favorite lamps called for a strong response, right? So I took a deep breath and let my sons have it: "Nobody hurt."

Just two little words. Yet they contained the constancy of my grandma's understanding and forgiveness. And most of all, they conveyed her unconditional love.

Love is patient, love is kind. It

does not envy, it does not boast,

it is not proud. It is not rude, it

is not self-seeking, it is not easily

angered, it keeps no record of

wrongs. Love does not delight in

evil but rejoices with the truth. It

always protects, always trusts,

always hopes, always perseveres.

—1 Corinthians 13: 4–7

My loving grandma,

I don't know anyone who loves better than you.
Your love is all-encompassing—you don't leave
anyone out, and yet you make me feel like I have
all of your love. How do you do that? I hope to
learn as I follow your example of kindness,
patience, and humility. Your love has enriched
my life more than you can know.

Your devoted grandchild

Grandma

Giving is the way you are,

Remembering those near and far.

Always loving in your own way,

Never ceasing night or day.

Doing, listening, or just being there,

Making others feel your tender care.

Another person could never be

    The **GRANDMA** and friend

    you are to me!

you

You've given me a foundation
of love and trust on
which to build my life.

Grandma

What one loves in childhood
stays in the heart forever.

Mary Jo Putney

Golden Moments

Jay stood on the deck of the navy ship in a rare moment of solitude and reflected on last night's attack from the enemy. He had joined the military for a tour in Vietnam—after all, his six older brothers were enlisted, and a good friend had recently died here—but never had the reality of war weighed so heavily on his eighteen-year-old heart.

Last night when his ship was being bombarded by enemy fire, he felt so vulnerable and helpless that he did the only thing he knew to do—he prayed the Lord's Prayer, and he prayed it like never before.

Now, feeling the breeze on his face and realizing anew the preciousness of life, the Lord's Prayer filled his mind again, mingling with thoughts of the summer he was ten. The memories unfolded like pages of an old photograph album.

Every summer since he was seven, Jay and his mom had driven the hundreds of miles from their home in northern California down to the small town where his grandma lived. His anticipation would grow as if it were the week before Christmas. But visiting Grandma even beat Christmas because it lasted much longer than one day.

The bird-of-paradise plants lining the driveway always greeted Jay with their pointy orange beaks, and the familiar palm tree waved its fronds in the front yard. The two orange trees stood sentinel in the side yard, not far from the sprawling rhubarb plants. Jay's mouth watered just thinking about the sweet, tart rhubarb sauce his grandma made.

As soon as the car came to a stop, Jay leaped out and ran into the house—through the living room, through the kitchen that was barely bigger than its red Formica table, and into Grandma's familiar bedroom, which also served as her sitting area. He found her just where he knew he would—in her gold recliner, the place her ample size felt most comfortable. The floor lamp shed its glow on her and the twin bed on the other side of her chair.

Her face broke into a grin when she saw Jay. "There's my boy!" She opened her arms wide for a hug.

"Hi, Grandma! I'm so glad we're finally here!" Her solid embrace and familiar scent filled him with contentment and joy.

Jay explored his summer home while his mom and grandma chattered away in the bedroom. He checked out the green shed behind the house, greeted Boots, the neighborhood cat, and toured the yards and his room. Jay ended up back in the living room where he stretched out on the brown, patterned rug.

His eyes fell on the corner china hutch, and yep, it was still in there: the lifeguard tower he had constructed out of Popsicle sticks the previous summer. Already, Jay knew it was going to be another special visit.

That evening Jay's mom bought some Chinese take-out food for dinner. In between bites of egg roll and chow mein, Jay and his grandma discussed the weeks ahead. Yes, Jay would get a summer pass for the YMCA pool. And he would go to the Boys Club he had frequented the year before. Jay wondered if Mike and Steve, his buddies from last summer, would be there again.

Grandma interrupted his thoughts. "Of course, you'll be going again to Vacation Bible School at my church. Several children have been asking about you. I can tell they are eager to see you." Jay grinned. Last year VBS had been a favorite part of his summer, with all the great games, stories, and refreshments.

The next morning Jay's mom departed, and the summer routine began. Because of her large size, it was hard for Grandma to get around; so Jay worked on the projects she had been saving for him. "The first thing I need you to do is shake out all the rugs and wash the windows. We need to let summer come into this place."

Jay's grandma expressed appreciation for every little thing he did, often saying, "You're the best grandson any grandma could have!" Sometimes she even gave him a dime for ice cream at the corner store.

On Sundays after church, they ate TV dinners of fried chicken. If watermelons went on sale for four cents a pound, they devoured several slices for supper when it was too hot to cook. And under the starry sky, they'd have Jay's favorite—a bowl of vanilla ice milk with rhubarb sauce or thin ribbons of chocolate syrup.

At bedtime Jay would watch his grandma comb out her long white hair that she kept coiled in a bun during the day. The tortoise-shell comb matched her warm, brown eyes.

"Jay," she said one night, "now that you're ten, I'm thinking that this is the summer to teach you something you need to learn. It's something you'll remember all your life."

Jay wondered what she meant and listened attentively as she went on. "I know you memorize Bible verses at VBS, but I'd like to be the one to teach you the Lord's Prayer."

At the foot of his grandma's recliner, under the soft shadow of the lamp, Jay sat and listened to the words as rich as his grandmother's voice. "Our Father who art in heaven, hallowed be thy name." Night after night, line by line, Jay memorized the prayer. When he learned a line perfectly, his grandma rewarded him with a treasured piece of Whitman's candy.

When they came to "Give us this day our daily bread," his grandma tilted her head to the side like she did when she had something important to say. "Jay, every time you say those words, 'Give us this day,' I want you to remember that's all we get—this day. Don't worry about yesterday; don't worry about tomorrow; just take care of today, and God will take care of you. There are 1,440 golden minutes in every day, and how you use them is entirely up to you."

Jay could tell that the glow on his grandma's face wasn't just from the lamplight. It came from deep inside, and it warmed him that night as well.

When Jay recited the entire prayer perfectly without a pause, Grandma gave him two pieces of Whitman's candy. Then she cupped her hands gently under his chin and looked deep into his eyes. "That prayer will stay with you all your life, my dear grandson, and you don't have to be in church to say it. God listens to us wherever we are, and He will always hear your every prayer."

Of all the golden summers at Grandma's house, Jay recalled that one the most vividly.

Before he left to go overseas, Jay had received a letter from his grandma.

> You know I will be praying for you every day.
> Don't forget all you've learned over the years, and
> especially rely on the strength of the Lord's Prayer.
> It will help see you through the hardest of times.

Last night, in the uncertainty and terror of war, Jay had found his grandmother's words to be true.

As his deployment continued, Jay found that whatever happened, it only further confirmed what his grandma had told him. When he was stuck below the water line in the hull of the ship, with shrapnel hits pounding like thunder, Jay discovered how many times he could say the Lord's Prayer in a matter of minutes.

Reciting those words comforted him on the lonely nights when he stood watch in the midnight hour, surrounded by the inky darkness of water and sky. And when he had to gather the bodies of his comrades to bring them home, he prayed from a place deep within that he hadn't known before.

Three years of duty in Vietnam brought many painful sights and troubling memories. Yet the Lord's Prayer and his grandma's words remained with him: "There are 1,440 golden minutes in every day, and how you use them is entirely up to you."

During the war and in the years that followed, Jay learned the art of treasuring golden moments—looking for something special in each day, whether it was a serene sunset, a child's smile, or the first bloom on the Christmas cactus his grandma had given him when he returned home from Vietnam.

Today Jay is a social worker, helping others to capture the sparkling gifts of each day's moments. And as a grandfather himself, he recently brought two grandchildren into his home to raise. Jay feels up to the challenge, though, and his radiant face matches the fervor in his voice when he talks about his twelve-year-old grandson who has an attention deficit disorder. "I just taught him the Lord's Prayer, and he knows every word, especially the part beginning 'Give us this day.' I told him the same words my grandma told me. It was the best of golden moments."

Ten Things My Grandmother Taught Me

1 The 23rd Psalm

2 How to play Yahtzee

3 How to knit

April 9, 2003

...w,
...y your mother told me of her
... I was taken with surprise,
...uy you were born and I first
...eyes you you I was taken by
...e again. I didn't think my
...ould be any fuller. You have
...t so much joy to our family
...om + Dad, your PaPa and me,
...our Aunt Carmen have been so
... blessed in the three years you've
...in our lives. And even though you
...a surprise to us, you were never
...surprise to your heavenly Father. He's
...you in his heart since the
...sinning of time. I pray you'll always
...ep this close to your heart.
                          Love,
                          Grandma

4 That a handwritten letter never goes out of style

5 How much milk is needed to fix too-thick cake frosting (very little!)

6 That one is never too old, too busy, or too hurried to help someone else

7 That it's best to do the dishes right after the meal

8 That sometimes what's needed most is a hug

9 That a filled candy jar on the coffee table says, "I love you"

10 How to flip pancakes

thank

you...

for being my biggest fan.

A Way with Words

Grandma always had a way of wrapping me up in her warm words, just as if she had pulled one of her cozy quilts around me. When I was little, she exclaimed over my drawings and hung them on her refrigerator. She attended my plays and concerts and declared that I was "the best." When she learned that my science project had won a blue ribbon, she called to tell me congratulations and how smart I was.

The words I remember most, however, are the ones she wrote to me. She added a personal note in each birthday card, writing about some good quality she saw in me. When I turned thirteen, she penned a prayer for my teen years, asking God to guide my every step and to grow me into a young woman with a pure and compassionate heart. After my first boyfriend broke up with me, she wrote me a note of comfort . . . and gave me chocolates!

How do I recall her words these many years later? In my cedar chest, tied with a pink satin ribbon, is every beloved card and letter. On dreary days I untie the ribbon and read again her warm words of affirmation. And I wonder about today's young generation. E-mail and phone calls are good things, yes—but it's the written word that will stay wrapped around children's hearts as they read them again on some distant rainy day.

My wise and wonderful grandma must have known that.

One generation will commend
your works to another; they will
tell of your mighty acts. They will
speak of the glorious splendor of
your majesty, and I will meditate
on your wonderful works.

—Psalm 145:4–5

My wonderful grandma,

   I have learned so much from the richness of your life. I've grown up hearing your stories of hope and heartache, and I know all of those things have made you the amazing person you are today. Thank you for telling me your stories; they inspire me and give me courage and wisdom for my journey.

Your indebted grandchild

You always make me feel
like you have all the time
in the world for me.

Grandma

Being pretty on the inside
means you don't hit your brother and
you eat all your peas
—that's what my grandma taught me.

Elizabeth Heller

Grandma Cookie

Before Jenna could even really talk, she had attached a name to her grandmother who lived nearby—Grandma Cookie. The title fit her as perfectly as Jenna's hand fit in the cookie jar. A visit to see Grandma Cookie—GC for short—always yielded a hug and a yummy treat from the cookie jar perched on the white-tiled counter.

For as long as she could remember, Jenna had been her grandma's little cookie maker. Sometimes her family would call her JC for Jenna Cookie, but Jenna didn't mind. She loved baking with Grandma.

At first Jenna had stood on a stepstool with an apron tied under her arms. Dropping the globs of chocolate chip cookie dough on the silver baking sheet filled her with pleasure, as did nibbling the chocolate chips that "escaped" the mixture. She criss-crossed the tops of peanut butter cookies with a fork and shaped balls the size of walnuts for the gingersnaps, rolling them in sugar before placing them on the tray. Before long her efforts started producing evenly sized cookies like her grandma made.

Often GC brewed a pot of tea, and Jenna added lots of milk and a spoonful of sugar to hers. Then came the best part of making cookies with Grandma—the conversation. The subjects were as seasonal as the cookies they made together.

In the fall, Jenna told her grandma about her new teacher, the kids in her class, and her soccer team. The Christmas season invited secrets between the two of them as they decorated cutout stars and angels and schemed surprises for her parents and her twin baby brother and sister. Spring blossomed with discussions about her science project and plans for summer vacation.

In the summer they baked early in the day or made no-bake cookies. Jenna kept her grandma informed of her swim team's schedule and reported on the out-of-town meets GC didn't get to see. Laughter flavored those times as much as ginger and cinnamon flavored the cookies.

Grandma Cookie often remarked, "Jenna, you and I are so much alike, I think we were made from the same cookie cutter." Jenna giggled as she tried to imagine a cookie cutter that could capture her grandma's curly, salt-and-pepper hair and one that would show her own long, blond hair that was often pulled back in a ponytail. No, they didn't look much alike, but like Grandma always said, "Our hearts were made from the same mold." Jenna liked the thought of that. Her grandma's heart was as sweet as the cookies she made.

Now that Jenna was older, the conversation had changed too. She'd lay a magazine photo by her grandma's teacup and ask, "GC, how do you think this hair style would look on me?" Or she'd model her outfit and say, "Mom doesn't like these jeans on me. What do you think?"

Before long the topic would turn to boys. "I like Kyle, but I can't tell if he likes me. What should I do?" Jenna loved how Grandma Cookie often paused before she spoke, as if a prayer preceded her answer. Her hazel eyes always shone with the same love Jenna heard in her words.

Grandma was the first to hear about the new girl at Jenna's school. "Victoria is so cool, GC. She wears all the latest styles, and I can tell the boys think she's really cool too. I can't believe she has chosen me to be one of her best friends!"

Grandma Cookie leaned across the kitchen table and put her hand over Jenna's. "And what is she like on the inside, JC? All I'm hearing about is what's on the outside. You and I know that the prettiest of cookies can be doughy and yucky on the inside if we don't take care what goes in them and how we bake them."

Jenna tossed her head. "You don't understand, Grandma. Victoria has lived in the big city most of her life, and she just knows more than the rest of us here in rinky-dink Meadow Valley. It's fun and exciting to be her friend."

"Just be careful, my dear Jenna. Don't forget who you are. Don't ever stop being your own special self."

Her grandma's words had faded by the following day when Victoria asked Jenna to go with her to the local drugstore to pick out some new makeup. Jenna was thrilled, and she and Victoria walked downtown right after school. They chatted about the hard math test that day, which boys were cutest, and the upcoming Christmas holidays.

"I guess I'll be going back to the city to have Christmas with my dad," Victoria said.

"Your parents are divorced?" This was the first time Jenna had heard any mention of Victoria's family.

"Yeah, but that's OK. This way I'll get twice the presents!" With a flick of her hair and an almost too bright smile, Victoria pushed open the glass door to the drugstore, and Jenna followed her inside.

They had just started looking at all the lipsticks when Jenna heard familiar voices—her kid brother and sister. "Hi, Jenna!" Their faces smiled up at her as she turned to look. "We just came from Grandma Cookie's, and she told us to tell you that this Saturday is the day to decorate all the cutout sugar cookies."

Victoria snickered. "Grandma Cookie?"

Jenna's little brother looked up at Victoria, apparently missing the tone of derision in her voice. "Yep, that's what Jenna named her when she was little. We call her GC for short. And Jenna is JC for Jenna Cookie."

This time Victoria burst out laughing. "How sweet. Oh, I just made a joke—get it? Cookies are sweet, and so are your names! I wouldn't let too many kids at school know about this other identity though, Jenna. It could ruin your reputation of being cool."

Jenna's cheeks flamed. She turned to say something to her brother, but he and her sister had disappeared. Taking a deep breath, she turned back to the glass shelves. "So, Victoria, what makeup do you want to buy?"

Victoria glanced around and in a low voice said, "Actually, I'm not planning to buy anything. I'm just going to put a couple of things in my coat pockets while you keep watch for me."

Jenna's stomach lurched, and her grandmother's words echoed in her ears: *"Just be careful, Jenna. Don't forget who you are."* Grandma's warning whirled with Vicoria's words in Jenna's mind, tearing away the veil of deception. How could she have been so blind? Her words poured out in a fierce whisper. "What kind of a person do you think I am? A thief? I thought you were so cool. Now I know better."

Jenna spun around and strode for the exit. Outside, she found her legs taking her up the hilly street through swirling snow to Grandma Cookie's house. When she arrived, her grandma took one look at her and pulled her inside and into her arms.

"Oh, Grandma, you were so right." Jenna's agitated words tumbled out as she relayed the afternoon's events. Grandma Cookie listened, only nodding her head now and then, and Jenna's stormy emotions were soon quieted by her grandmother's warm and calming presence. Jenna fell into a reflective silence as they sat side by side on the couch under a cozy quilt, her head on Grandma's shoulder.

"You know what, GC?" Jenna spoke quietly now. "I feel sorry for Victoria. I thought she was so cool . . ." Her voice trailed off.

"When really," her grandmother said softly, "she's a lonely, hurting girl who probably envies the fact that you have a close, loving family."

Jenna looked up at her as understanding filled her heart and mind. "That's why she laughed, isn't it? You always say, 'You either laugh or you cry.' I think she really wanted to cry."

Grandma returned her gaze with that signature look of affirming love.

An idea hit so fast that it sat Jenna straight up. "Grandma, would it be all right if I invited Victoria to decorate cookies with us Saturday?"

Her grandmother's quick smile gave Jenna her answer.

"I have something for you, Jenna, and I think this is the best time to give it to you. Think of it as an early Christmas present, because you just gave me the best gift I could ask for."

She stood up, opened a cupboard, and drew out a large item wrapped in layers of red tissue paper and tied with a shimmering silver bow. "Remember how I've often said that we're made from the same cookie cutter because we're so much alike? And how you've told me it would be impossible to find a cookie cutter that looks like both of us? Well, I think I've found the solution. Open it, JC."

Jenna peeled off the layers of paper and pulled out the biggest heart-shaped cookie cutter she had ever seen. She smiled, but she knew her puzzlement showed.

"Big hearts, Jenna. God gave us the same big hearts to love other people." Grandma Cookie reached over and hugged her. "And you just showed me the size of yours."

Grandma's Crinkle Gingersnaps

Combine:

  $1^1/_8$ to $1^1/_4$ cups oil

  $^1/_2$ cup molasses

  2 eggs

  2 cups sugar

Add:

  4 cups flour

  $^1/_2$ tsp. salt

  4 tsp. baking soda

  2 tsp. ground ginger

  2 tsp. ground cinnamon

  2 tsp. ground cloves

Chill. Preheat oven to 350 degrees. Roll cookie dough into balls the size of a large walnut, then roll in sugar. Place on ungreased cookie sheet and bake for 10–12 minutes. Makes approximately five dozen cookies, three inches in diameter.

Ten Reasons Grandma
Is So Grand

1 She still has the
Christmas ornaments
I made for her in
grade school.

2 She knows me better
than I know myself . . .
and still loves me.

3 She brags about
me to her friends
(and anyone else
who will listen).

4 She lets me eat
dessert first!

5 She's never in too big a
hurry to have time for me.

6 *She's convinced I'm the best.*

7 *I can tell her anything.*

8 *She really listens to me and hears my heart.*

9 *She's always willing to do anything for me.*

10 *Even now, she keeps the latest photograph of me on her fridge.*

thank

you...

*for enriching my life with your wisdom,
your laughter, and your love.*

The Flavor of Love

I stood in front of the foggy freezer cases in the supermarket after work, scanning the tempting titles of ice cream: almond praline, double fudge brownie, peaches and cream. I looked for my favorite—mocha almond fudge—but in my search, my eyes froze on the pink label of peppermint.

An hour later I sat curled up on my couch eating a bowl of peppermint ice cream and traveling down memory lane. I saw myself the summer I turned eight, meandering down the main street of Disneyland with my grandmother. My fun and loving grandma was all mine for the day, and I felt like Cinderella. We stopped at the ice cream parlor and ordered peppermint, the flavor that matched the striped wallpaper. Grandma and I talked and laughed over each pink spoonful.

My mental wanderings took me to other tasty times, like when Grandma taught me how to make creamy hot vanilla pudding, adding chocolate chips that melted in the pudding and in my mouth. I saw again her candy dish, always offering a welcome in the form of my favorite treats: rootbeer barrels, soft caramels, and chocolate mints. And I could almost taste the toast smeared with lavish helpings of her homemade strawberry preserves, which I had named Grammy Jam.

Lingering over my ice cream, I smiled at all the delicious memories. Most of all, I relished the remembrance of the one flavor Grandma always added to everything—the flavor of love.

A word aptly spoken is like apples

of gold in settings of silver.

—Proverbs 25:11

Dear Grandma,

When I think of you, I remember all the kind, uplifting words you have spoken to me over the years. Words that made me smile, words that dried my tears, words that made me want to be a better person. Your words of affirmation and care have truly been a gift to me, like splashes of sunshine in my life.

Your listening grandchild

Dear heavenly Father,

Thank You for my dear grandma. Thank You for the joy she brings to my life by the way she takes joy in me. Thank You for her wisdom and insights that light the paths of my life. Thank You for her understanding and patience that bring a calming presence wherever she goes. Thank You for the music of her laughter, the lilt in her voice, and the glow on her face that warms everyone around her.

Thank You for the gift of Grandma and the love she so freely gives to all. Thank You for the example she is to me of Your unconditional love. Above all, thank You that I am the one so blessed to call her not only my grandmother but also my treasured friend.

Amen